A Damn Close-Run Thing

A BRIEF HISTORY OF THE FALKLANDS CONFLICT

RUSSELL PHILLIPS

SHILKA PUBLISHING

WWW.SHILKA.CO.UK

Shilka Publishing
Apt 2049
Chynoweth House
Trevissome Park
Truro
TR4 8UN
www.shilka.co.uk

Book Layout ©2013 BookDesignTemplates.com

Ordering Information:
Quantity sales. Special discounts are available on quantity purchases by corporations, associations, and others. For details, contact the "Special Sales Department" at the address above.

A Damn Close-Run Thing/ Russell Phillips. —1st ed.
ISBN 978-0-9927648-6-9

Contents

It was a damn close-run thing.

—Major-General Moore, commander of the British land forces
in the South Atlantic

[1]

Introduction

Author's note: unless specified otherwise, times are always given in the local time zone.

The Falkland Islands are an archipelago consisting of two large islands (West Falkland and East Falkland), and 776 smaller islands. The islands are situated roughly 250 nautical miles east of southern Argentina, in the South Atlantic. South Georgia is a large island around 700 nautical miles east-southeast of the Falkland Islands. The South Sandwich Islands are a chain of small islands 280 nautical miles southeast of South Georgia.

In 1982, Argentina and the United Kingdom had both claimed sovereignty over the Falkland Islands (referred to as Islas Malvinas by the Argentinians) and their dependencies, South

Georgia and the South Sandwich Islands, for over 150 years. At the time of the Falklands Conflict, most Britons were only vaguely aware of the islands' existence, but the Argentinians felt it was an issue of great importance and national pride. One Argentinian army officer said, "We viewed the Malvinas as a lost treasure with a sentimental longing that everyone in Argentina shared."

[2]

Historical Context

To properly understand the 1982 Falklands Conflict between Argentina and the United Kingdom, it is useful to have some understanding of the historical context.

The dispute between the UK and Argentina over sovereignty of the Falkland Islands dates back to 1816, when Argentina declared its independence from Spain, which had previously claimed sovereignty over the islands. In 1945, Argentina brought its claim to the newly-formed United Nations, thus raising international awareness of the issue. The UK offered to take the matter to mediation in the International Court of Justice in the Hague in 1947, 1948, and 1955, but Argentina declined the offers, saying that the court did not have jurisdiction to rule on the matter. The UK unilaterally submitted the case to the court in 1955, but the case was removed from the court's lists the following year, after Argentina stated that they would not accept the court's decision. Also in 1955, Argentina set up a small station named Teniente Esquivel on Thule, one of the South Sandwich Islands, but this was evacuated a year later.

In 1964, the United Nations passed a resolution calling on the UK and Argentina to find a peaceful resolution to the sovereignty dispute, bearing in mind the interests of the islanders. Argentina has always argued that the islanders are not indigenous and were brought in to replace the Argentinian population that was expelled after the re-establishment of British rule in 1833, and therefore have no right to self-determination.

In 1966, 20 armed Argentinian revolutionaries hijacked a DC-4 aircraft and forced the pilot to land on the racecourse at Stanley (the capital of the Falkland Islands), where they took four islanders hostage. The Falkland Islands Defence Force (FIDF) and local Royal Marines detachment kept the aircraft and hijackers contained. The hijackers surrendered with no loss of life, and were returned to Argentina. In November 1968, a light aircraft from Argentina landed on Eliza Cove Road outside Stanley, prompting a similar alert, but the passengers were unarmed Argentinian journalists.

In 1976, an Argentinian gunboat fired upon a British Antarctic Survey ship. In November of that year, a party from the Argentine Air Force landed on Thule and set up a small military base with barracks, helicopter landing pad, radio station, and flagpole, from which they flew the Argentinian flag. The new base, named Corbeta Uruguay, was not publicly announced, but was discovered by the British a month later. The British government made a number of official protests, but the base remained in Argentinian hands until after the Falklands Conflict.

In 1977, the Argentinian navy cut off the fuel supply to Port Stanley Airport. The UK government, concerned that Argentina might mount an armed expedition, dispatched a nuclear submarine (HMS Dreadnought) and two frigates (HMS Alacrity and Phoebe). These deployments were discreetly leaked to the Argentinian government, but not made public until some years later.

Meanwhile, Argentina and the UK had held a series of talks between 1964 and 1981, and some progress was made in establishing links between the islands and Argentina. Regular flights between Argentina and the islands were established, and the Argentinian national oil and gas company started to supply the islands. However, there was no progress on the central issue of sovereignty. The islanders, believing that the greater links to Argentina were the first steps towards Argentinian sovereignty, set up a group to lobby the UK parliament on their behalf. Just as Argentina refused to recognise the islanders' right to self-determination, successive UK governments, under intense lobbying, maintained a position that the wishes of the islanders were paramount. Since neither government was willing or able to change their fundamental position, further progress was not possible.

THE 1980S

In 1980, Nicholas Ridley, the Minister of State for the newly-elected Conservative government, travelled to the Falkland Islands to put a proposal to the islanders which would see sovereignty transferred to Argentina, but with the islands leased back to the UK, and under UK control, for a fixed term (100 years was suggested), after which Argentina would take over. He was given a cool reception, and the islanders roundly rejected the proposal.

In 1981, the British Nationality Act was passed, which removed British citizenship from many islanders. As part of a program of defence cuts, it was announced that the ice-breaker HMS Endurance (the only permanent Royal Navy presence in the South Atlantic) was to be scrapped. These cuts also required the decommissioning of the aircraft carrier HMS Hermes, and the aircraft carrier HMS Invincible was due to be sold to Australia. These developments convinced the ruling military junta in Argentina that the UK would not oppose a military takeover of the islands, which they hoped would divert public opinion from various problems at home, and so they made plans for an invasion, to take place in 1982.

In December 1981, an Argentinian named Constantino Davidoff paid £160,000 for the rights to dismantle and salvage scrap metal from the now-defunct whaling stations on South Georgia. When he enquired about hiring Argentinian naval vessels for transport, he became an unwitting part of the plan to take the Falkland Islands. On the 17th of March 1982, he and 41 workers landed at Leith, without a landing permit, and without alerting the British Antarctic Survey (BAS) base at Grytviken.

Two days later, they were spotted by members of the BAS, who reported that some of the men were in military uniform, and an Argentinian flag was flying from a building. Governor Hunt, based at Stanley in the Falklands, sent a message to the Argentinians, informing them that they had landed illegally, and ordering them to board their ship and report to the base commander at Grytviken for further instructions. Meanwhile, HMS Endurance was ordered to South Georgia, with a detachment of Royal Marines on board.

Concerned that the Argentinians might be planning to invade the Falkland Islands, the British government decided to send some nuclear-powered submarines to the area at the end of March 1982. The nuclear powered Swiftsure-class submarine HMS Spartan was the first to arrive in the area, on the 12th of April, and she was joined by her sister, HMS Splendid, on the 19th. HMS Conqueror had just started a planned period of maintenance when she received her war orders on the 30th of March. The maintenance was hurriedly cancelled, and she set sail on the 4th of April, with 14 men of 6 SBS (Special Boat Squadron) embarked. She arrived in the South Atlantic on the 16th, two weeks after the invasion.

[3]

Operation Azul

Spurred on in part by anti-government feeling, including riots and strikes, the Argentine junta brought forward their plans to invade the Falklands, and on the 28th of March, troops started boarding transport ships. The Argentinian submarine ARA Santa Fe, with 13 members of the elite tactical divers group embarked, carried out reconnaissance of Port William on the 31st of March.

The British had detected the invasion fleet's departure, and on the afternoon of the 1st of April Governor Hunt received a telegram from the Foreign and Commonwealth Office in the UK, warning that an Argentinian task force could attack Stanley at dawn the next day. The timing meant that the Royal Marine garrison was larger than usual, since it was in the process of changing over, and both the old and new garrisons were present. Consequently, there were 85 Royal Marines on the islands, with 25 men of the Falkland Islands Defence Force, although some retired members of the FIDF also reported for duty, so that around 40 men were available from the FIDF.

At 23:00 on the 1st of April (04:00 on the 2nd of April UK time), an Argentinian force of marines and special forces landed at Lake Point, south of Stanley. The force split up, with the majority heading to Moody Brook Barracks (which, unbeknown to the Argentinians, was deserted), with the rest heading for Government House.

At 04:30 on the 2nd of April, ARA Santa Fe landed her advance force in Yorke Bay. They planted beacons to guide the main force, then advanced on Port Stanley Airport. Meeting no resistance, they quickly secured both the airport and the lighthouse.

At around 06:00, the first Argentinians arrived at Government House and started to attack. They were later reinforced by the troops that had initially gone to Moody Brook Barracks. LVTP-7 amphibious assault vehicles started landing north of Stanley from 06:30, and from 06:45, troops started to arrive at Port Stanley Airport by helicopter.

At 08:00, Governor Hunt sent a deputy to find the Argentinian command post in the town hall and initiate negotiation of surrender terms. Although the commander of the Royal Marines had advised that they could escape out of Stanley with Governor Hunt and set up a seat of government elsewhere, the British forces surrendered at 09:30. A section of Royal Marines was still at large, but decided to destroy and bury their weapons before surrendering, to avoid any civilian loss of life.

After the surrender, photographs and video were taken of the Royal Marines and FIDF, laying face-down in a field. This was intended to demonstrate that there were no casualties among the defending forces, but when the footage was shown on British TV, it galvanised public opinion against the invasion. The Royal Marines were returned to the UK via Uruguay, while the members of the FIDF were disarmed and most were allowed to return home, though some were placed under house arrest.

SOUTH GEORGIA

The Royal Marines on South Georgia heard on the 2nd of April that the Falkland Islands had been invaded and made plans to defend Grytviken until nightfall, then use the cover of darkness to retreat and start a guerrilla campaign. The beach was mined, and improvised explosive devices were rigged on the jetty and in some of the buildings. HMS Endurance, heading towards South Georgia, passed on a message from London to the Royal Marines, instructing them to take no action that might endanger lives.

At 10:00 on the 3rd of April, the local Argentinian commander radioed the commander of the BAS station, Steve Martin, informing him that the Falkland Islands had surrendered, and suggesting that they do the same. A little later, the Argentinians radioed Martin again, ordering him to assemble everyone on the beach, as they were about to land troops. Martin replied that such a landing would be illegal and would be met with military action. At this point, Lieutenant Keith Mills, commander of the Royal Marine detachment on the island, took over command from Martin. The commander of HMS Endurance, having picked up the Argentinian message, sent a radio message to Martin releasing him from his previous rules of engagement, and ordering him to "defend if provoked", but this message was not received.

At 12:00, the survey ship ARA Bahia Paraiso and corvette ARA Guerrico sailed into Cumberland East Bay and launched two helicopters, carrying 22 marines. One helicopter was shot down by the Royal Marines, with the loss of two men dead and several injured. As the Argentinian marines advanced, ARA Guerrico came closer to shore and bombarded the defenders with her 100mm gun. The Royal Marines opened fire on ARA Guerrico, and hit her on the waterline with a Carl Gustav anti-tank rocket. Taking on water, with her 100mm gun and one of the 40mm guns out of action, ARA Guerrico retreated out of the bay, but suffered more hits from small arms and anti-tank rockets as she left.

HMS Endurance had now arrived back in the area and dispatched one of her helicopters to find out what was happening, which arrived in time to see the corvette leaving the bay. The crew asked for permission to engage, which was refused, since Endurance's orders were to stay 150 miles from South Georgia and not to fire unless provoked.

Meanwhile, more Argentinian marines had been ferried ashore by helicopter, and as ARA Guerrico started to shell the Royal Marine positions from a position out of range of return fire,

Lieutenant Mills decided to surrender before suffering pointless losses.

Mills approached the Argentinian forces on shore under a white flag, and explained that he wished to surrender. The commander of the Argentinian forces, Lieutenant Commander Alfredo Astiz, came ashore to accept the surrender. The Argentinians treated their captives with respect, and provided the sole Royal Marine casualty with medical care.

The Royal Marines and BAS team were transported to Argentina, where Mills and Martin agreed to be interviewed by a panel of senior naval officers about the conduct of the Argentinian forces during the invasion. The whole party were then flown to Uruguay and handed over to the British embassy, where arrangements were made for them to be flown back to the UK.

Pebble Island

On the 23rd of April, an Argentinian aircraft landed on the airstrip on Pebble Island, north of West Falkland, apparently to deliver mail. One of the occupants surveyed the airstrip—then some hours later, a helicopter landed an Argentinian patrol. The patrol marched into the settlement, confiscating all radio transmitters.

From then on, the local population were largely confined to their houses by the Argentinian garrison.

The Argentinians established an air base on Pebble Island, with T-34C-1 Turbo Mentor and FMA IA 58 Pucará ground attack aircraft. A base with 400 men was planned, though by the time of the SAS (Special Air Service) attack, only about 150 men were deployed on the base.

[4]

Occupation

On the 3rd of April 1982, the Argentine junta named Brigadier General Mario Menéndez the "Military Governor of the Malvinas, South Georgia, and the South Sandwich Islands". When Argentinian military police arrived, they quickly deported several outspoken critics of Argentina, though later they changed their policy, detaining people at Fox Bay instead.

Although there were some isolated incidents of bad treatment, and some islanders were imprisoned as potential troublemakers, the islanders were generally treated with respect, in accordance with instructions from Brigadier General Menéndez. The Argentinians were still hoping that the British government would not oppose the new rulers of the islands, and believed that treating the islanders with respect would make this more likely.

The Argentinians imposed various new rules. Spanish became the official language, and Stanley's name was changed to Puerto Argentino. Traffic was ordered to drive on the right, though some islanders continued to drive on the left in an act of civil disobedience. The FIDF was declared illegal, the Falkland Islands pound was replaced by the Argentinian peso, and stamps were franked with an Islas Malvinas postmark.

[5]

Response to the Invasion

When the victory was announced in Argentina, the streets of Buenos Aires were filled with happy people waving Argentinian flags, chanting "Viva Argentina!" and "Viva las Malvinas!" Only a week before, Buenos Aires had been paralysed by a general strike and the same streets had been filled with rioters. General Galtieri announced on radio and television, "Let the nation understand the profound and ineluctable national feeling of this decision so that the collective sense of responsibility and effort can accompany this task and allow, with the help of God, the legitimate rights of the Argentinian people, postponed prudently and patiently for 150 years, to become a reality."

Following the news of the invasion in Britain, the Foreign Secretary, Lord Carrington, resigned, and Secretary of State for Defence John Nott offered his resignation, but it was refused. There was some doubt about whether or not Britain could retake the islands by force. Sir Henry Leach, First Sea Lord and Chief of the Naval Staff, was adamant that it could be done, but John Nott argued against it, as did the Chiefs of Staff of the Army and Royal Air Force. The decision was made to send a task force to re-take the islands, while simultaneously pursuing a diplomatic resolution. Nine Royal Navy ships on exercise in the Mediterranean were ordered south, and nuclear submarines were given orders to sail. The RAF deployed Vulcan bombers, Victor tankers and Phantom fighters to Ascension Island in preparation for the Black Buck bombing raids. Britain cut off diplomatic ties to Argentina, ordering Argentinian diplomats out of the country and freezing Argentinian assets in Britain.

An emergency debate was held in the British House of Commons on the 3rd of April. The government was strongly criticised for not anticipating the Argentinian invasion, but the decision to prepare a task force for invasion was endorsed. Although the British had no plans to attack the Argentinian mainland, hints were dropped to the media that Vulcan bombers might be used to attack bases in Argentina.

The submarines HMS Spartan and HMS Splendid were already en-route to the South Atlantic, having been dispatched when an invasion seemed likely. On the 4th of April, the submarine HMS Conqueror sailed from Faslane, and on the following day the aircraft carriers HMS Hermes and Invincible set sail from Portsmouth with the main part of the task force.

The cruise liner Canberra was requisitioned for use in the Falklands under the Ships Taken Up From Trade (STUFT) scheme, and she set sail with 3 Commando Brigade on board to join the rest of the task force. The United States Secretary of State, Alexander Haig, visited London and Buenos Aires in an effort to mediate a peaceful resolution, and the EEC imposed economic sanctions on Argentina.

On the 12th of April, as HMS Spartan arrived in the area, the British government declared a Maritime Exclusion Zone, covering an area with a radius of 200 nautical miles, centred on the Falkland Islands. Any Argentinian warship or naval auxiliary entering this zone would be liable to attack. On the 23rd of April, a message passed via the Swiss embassy in Buenos Aries to the Argentinian government clarified the British position, which was that any Argentinian warship posing a threat to British forces would be attacked.

The main British task force arrived at Ascension Island in the mid-Atlantic. A small force of two destroyers and a tanker were sent south to rendezvous with the submarine HMS Conqueror and the ice-breaker HMS Endurance. They were then to retake the island of South Georgia.

On the 30th of April, the Maritime Exclusion Zone was re-classified as a Total Exclusion Zone. Any sea vessel or aircraft entering the zone, from any country, was now liable to be attacked without warning. On the same day, US President Reagan put an end to the US-led mediation process, declaring support for Britain. The US imposed economic sanctions on Argentina, whilst offering Britain material and other aid. On the 7th of May, the British government extended the Total Exclusion Zone to within 12 nautical miles of the Argentinian coast. This effectively meant that any Argentinian ship or aircraft encountered outside Argentinian territorial waters was liable to be attacked.

There was widespread support for the UK position in the international community. As already noted, the EEC and United States supported the British position, albeit somewhat reluctantly in the case of the US. The UN Security Council passed Resolution 502 on the 3rd of April, which demanded immediate Argentinian withdrawal from the Islands. Many South American countries supported Argentina, and on the 28th of April, the Organisation of American States announced its support for Argentina's sovereignty claim, though it also called for peaceful negotiations.

DIPLOMATIC RESPONSE

The United States counted both the UK and Argentina as allies, and so both sides looked to them for support, putting them in a difficult position, and an internal split ensued. The Defence Department and the Pentagon supported the UK, while the State Department supported Argentina, fearing that South American countries would cease their backing of the administration's Central American policy if the United States supported the UK. When US efforts at mediation failed, they provided political support to the UK in the United Nations. They also discreetly provided logistical support on Ascension Island and military equipment such as the latest generation of the Sidewinder air-to-air missile, which were fitted to Sea Harriers.

France gave political and practical support to the UK. They provided Super Etendard and Mirage aircraft (the same models that they had earlier supplied to Argentina), along with pilots for Sea Harrier pilots to train against. Delivery of Exocet missiles to Argentina was immediately cancelled. Five missiles had already been delivered, but further deliveries were held back until hostilities ended. In addition, French intelligence worked with British intelligence to prevent Argentina acquiring more Exocet missiles on the international market. France supplied technical information about the Exocet, allowing British intelligence agents to covertly disable missiles that were being sold to Argentina, while other agents outbid Argentinian buyers trying to buy Exocets. The Exocet threat was considered so serious that the SBS were ordered to sink a merchant ship taking a delivery of the missiles to Argentina, though this operation was cancelled when it became clear that the ship would not arrive before hostilities ended.

New Zealand sent a ship to the Indian Ocean to relieve a British ship, freeing it for deployment to the South Atlantic, and Chile provided the UK with intelligence. The UK entered into negotiations with Chile to use a Chilean airfield as a base for Nimrod patrol aircraft, which would have helped make up for the UK's lack of satellite reconnaissance coverage in the South Atlantic. These negotiations were unsuccessful, but in his memoirs, Sir John Nott described Chilean help as "very valuable".

Most South American countries supported Argentina (Chile being a notable exception). Peru and Venezuela provided Argentina with logistical support, while Brazil leased two maritime patrol aircraft to Argentina. Israel and South Africa both provided Argentina with support; Israeli military advisers already in Argentina remained there so that they could provide assistance. The Soviet Union provided Argentina with military intelligence and satellite reconnaissance, and helped them to acquire man-portable surface-to-air missiles from Libya.

[6]

Operation Black Buck

Operations Black Buck 1 to 7 were a series of air raids against Argentinian positions in the Falkland Islands, using soon-to-be retired Vulcan bombers and Victor tankers, with Phantom fighters providing escorts. Three Vulcans and 11 Victors were flown to Ascension Island, from where the attacks would be launched. The Vulcans' in-flight refuelling systems had been blocked off and had to be re-enabled. In addition, electronic countermeasures (ECM) pods and inertial guidance systems were fitted to the aircraft. Since the Vulcan pilots had not practised in-air refuelling for some years, each Vulcan carried a senior air-to-air refuelling instructor from the Victor force, who would pilot the Vulcan when performing in-flight refuelling. Neither the Vulcans nor the Victors were intended for missions at such great distances, so the tankers as well as the bombers had to be refuelled in-flight. Each mission therefore presented significant logistical challenges, especially since there was only one runway on Ascension Island capable of launching either Vulcans or Victors.

Of the seven raids planned, five were carried out. For the first raid, two Vulcans took off, each carrying 21 1,000lb bombs. One had to return to Ascension shortly after take-off, but the other continued, dropping its bombs on Port Stanley airport early on the 1st of May. One bomb landed in the centre of the runway, while another damaged the control tower, and two personnel were killed. The runway was quickly repaired and in use by C-130 Hercules aircraft, though not by fast jets.

Two of the remaining missions were anti-radar missions using AGM-45 Shrike missiles supplied by the United States, which damaged a long-range radar and a fire-control radar. The other two completed missions were flown against Port Stanley airport and inflicted some damage.

[7]

ARA General Belgrano

The second largest ship in the Argentinian fleet was the ARA General Belgrano, a cruiser that had been bought from the U.S. Navy in 1951 (where it had been the USS Phoenix). She was armed with 15 six-inch guns, eight five-inch guns, and two British Sea Cat anti-aircraft missile systems.

On the 26th of April, she set sail with two destroyers as escort, the ARA Piedra Buena and ARA Bouchard. A few days later, the British nuclear submarine HMS Conqueror picked up the group on sonar and started to trail them. Conqueror had experienced some problems with her communication systems, but managed to get situation reports to Britain. The rules of engagement for the submarines stated that only the

29

Argentinian aircraft carrier, ARA Veinticinco de Mayo, and Argentinian submarines could be attacked outside the exclusion zone. HMS Conqueror, therefore, could not attack the Belgrano while she remained outside the exclusion zone.

Admiral Woodward, in command of the British task force, was anxious to have the Belgrano sunk, but had no authority to order an attack. An urgent request was sent to London for permission to attack the Belgrano, and on the 2nd of May the request was taken to Margaret Thatcher, the British Prime Minister. A decision was made around lunchtime. The Belgrano had been heading towards the exclusion zone, and the Conqueror had sailed into position to attack once the line was crossed, but at around 06:00 local time, the sonar operators on Conqueror realised that their target had changed course and was now heading away from the exclusion zone. They continued to tail the small group, and later in the day, received orders that the Belgrano was to be attacked.

At 12:57 on the 2nd of May, HMS Conqueror fired three Mark 8 torpedoes. The Mark 8s were old, unguided torpedoes, but had been chosen in preference to the newer, wire-guided Mark 24 torpedoes for two reasons: there were doubts about the newer model's reliability, and the older torpedo had a larger warhead, which was likely to be important, given that the Belgrano had a six-inch-thick belt of armour along the waterline. Two of the torpedoes hit, causing a great deal of damage and cutting all electrical power, causing the pumps to fail. Twenty minutes after the torpedoes hit, the order was given to abandon ship. Including two civilians, 323 men died in the attack, but 770 were rescued.

The sinking of the Belgrano was the cause of some controversy in Britain, partly due to early reports of very few survivors, and partly because she was outside the exclusion zone and sailing away from the islands at the time of the sinking. The controversy lasted throughout the conflict, and occasionally came up afterwards. In 1984 a senior civil servant at the Ministry of Defence leaked documents about the sinking of the Belgrano to a Labour MP. Some years later, the Belgrano's captain and the Argentinian government both stated that the sinking was a legitimate act of war.

[8]

Operation Algeciras

Operation Algeciras was an Argentinian operation to sink a British warship in Gibraltar. The intention was to make the British feel vulnerable in Europe, thus forcing the Royal Navy to keep some ships in Europe instead of sending them to the Falklands. Mounting the attack at a UK base would have had more impact, but was less likely to succeed. The operation was the brainchild of Admiral Jorge Anaya, part of the governing military junta in Argentina. Anaya kept the operation absolutely secret, even from other members of the government.

Four men were sent to Spain to carry out the attack, all former members of the Montoneros, a guerrilla group that had fought successive

Argentinian governments, and been one of the targets of the junta's Dirty War (the Montoneros claim 5,000 of their number were killed by the junta). That these men were willing to co-operate with a senior member of the junta in order to help Argentina keep the newly-acquired Falkland Islands is indicative of how strongly most Argentinians felt about their claim to sovereignty of the islands.

Italian limpet mines were shipped via diplomatic pouch to Spain, and the men were given false Argentinian passports, with stamps indicating that they had entered Spain earlier than was actually the case. False documents were used so that the Argentinian government could deny all knowledge of the operation, should it be compromised.

The four men flew to Malaga via Paris, then drove by car to Algeciras, with the limpet mines and diving equipment in the car boots. Having arrived in Algeciras, they spent some days watching the bay and port of Gibraltar. They bought an inflatable raft and fishing gear to provide a cover activity. Their plan, once a suitable target was spotted, was to enter the water at 18:00, plant mines around midnight, exit around 05:00 and drive to Barcelona.

The mines would be timed to explode as they started their drive away from the area.

Anaya refused permission to attack the first two potential targets. The first was a British minesweeper, and the second an oil tanker. Although sinking the oil tanker could have blocked the port, Anaya refused permission on the grounds that it was not flying a British flag, and so would likely outrage Spain, especially if the attack resulted in a major oil spill.

On the 2nd of May, the frigate HMS Ariadne arrived at Gibraltar. Anaya initially refused permission to attack because there was the real possibility of a peaceful resolution, but the sinking of ARA General Belgrano later that day made hostilities inevitable. On the 3rd of May the order was given to carry out the attack. The men requested that they be allowed to admit that they were working for the Argentinian navy, but this request was refused.

The owner of the car-hire business that had provided the men with one of their cars had become suspicious and informed the police. When two of the men went to renew the hire, the owner rang the police and kept the men occupied until police arrived and arrested them. Shortly after, the other two were arrested in their hotel. Despite their orders to the contrary, the men revealed that they were working for the Argentinian navy. The Spanish president, wanting to avoid tensions with the UK and Argentina, ordered that the men should be flown to the Canary Islands via Madrid, then put on an aeroplane to Buenos Aires.

[9]

Operation Paraquet

As the task force headed south, the UK government ordered them to retake South Georgia first. Although the military commanders argued that it would make more military sense to send the entire force straight to the Falkland Islands, the government wanted to be able to present an early victory to the public.

The nuclear submarine HMS Conqueror arrived off South Georgia on the 19th of April, and commenced patrolling. A Victor from Ascension Island flew a reconnaissance flight the next day. Neither HMS Conqueror nor the Victor found any enemy ships.

A small task group consisting of the destroyer HMS Antrim, frigate HMS Plymouth, ice-breaker

HMS Endurance, and RFA Tidespring headed for South Georgia, arriving on the 21st of April. On the 21st, men of the SAS and SBS were landed on South Georgia, but due to extreme weather had to be picked up again. Two Wessex helicopters were lost in the attempts to pick up the SAS, but eventually the SAS troopers and the aircrew from the crashed helicopters were picked up by the last Wessex. Despite being overloaded, Lieutenant Commander Stanley managed to pilot the helicopter through the atrocious weather back to HMS Antrim. Stanley was awarded the Distinguished Service Order for his skilful and courageous flying. Both the SAS and SBS later managed to land observation parties via Gemini boats. The frigate HMS Brilliant, carrying two Lynx helicopters, was detached from the main task force to reinforce the South Georgia group.

On the 24th of April, the Argentinian submarine Santa Fe arrived in Grytviken with a force of marines to reinforce the garrison. As she left on the 25th, she was spotted on the surface by a Wessex helicopter. She was attacked by several helicopters and forced to return to Grytviken, where her crew left her unmanned on the surface.

Despite the fact that many of the Royal Marines were on RFA Tidespring some distance away, the decision was made to make an immediate assault with a force scratched together from the men available. The force of three troops (72 men) and two Royal Artillery observers were landed by helicopter near Grytviken at 14:15 on the 25th of April. HMS Plymouth and Antrim fired in support, but deliberately missed Grytviken itself, simply making a demonstration of the fire power available. As the land force advanced on Grytviken and HMS Antrim sailed into Cumberland Bay, white flags were raised in Grytviken. The garrison surrendered at 17:15.

The commander of the operation sent a signal to London, stating, "Be pleased to inform Her Majesty that the White Ensign flies alongside the Union Jack in South Georgia. God save the Queen." John Nott and Margaret Thatcher appeared on the steps of number 10 Downing Street to announce the news to the media. Mrs Thatcher refused to answer questions, saying, "Just rejoice at that news and congratulate our forces and the marines."

On the 26th of April, the garrison at Leith was contacted by radio and invited to surrender, but they refused. However, when the SAS and Royal Marines arrived at Leith later in the day with HMS Endurance and Plymouth in support, the garrison surrendered without a fight.

[10]

HMS Sheffield

At 07:50 on the 4th of May, an Argentinian patrol aircraft picked up the British carrier battle group on its radar, 70 miles southeast of Stanley. Two Super Etendards were flown from Rio Grande at 09:45, each carrying a single Exocet anti-ship missile. After refuelling in-flight, they flew at low altitude, and received target information from the patrol aircraft. They increased height to scan with their radars, and having picked up targets, descended once more before releasing their missiles at a range of 20-30 miles.

HMS Sheffield's radar picked up the incoming missiles, but too late for any action to be taken. One missile impacted her amidships, around eight feet above the waterline. The other missile missed and hit the water half a mile off her port beam. Even though it didn't explode, the missile that hit started fires and fractured the water main, making fire-fighting difficult. Twenty of her crew died. The remainder were taken off and HMS Yarmouth took her under tow. The high seas caused flooding through the impact hole, and HMS Sheffield sank on the 10th of May, the first Royal Navy vessel to be sunk in action since World War II.

The sinking of HMS Sheffield led to a new policy, which stated that any Royal Navy ship that thought it may be under missile attack was to turn towards the threat, accelerate to maximum speed, and fire chaff. This manoeuvre was to be initiated as soon as emissions from the Super Etendard's radar were picked up.

[11]

Narwal

On the 9th of May, a pair of Sea Harriers detected the 1,500 ton Narwal, an Argentinian fish factory ship suspected of acting as an intelligence trawler. They strafed and bombed the ship, managing to stop her, but she didn't sink. An SBS team was dispatched on two Sea King helicopters.

Using an assault technique intended for maritime anti-terrorism work, the SBS abseiled onto the ship in heavy seas. They quickly took control of the Narwhal and moved the crew onto the Sea Kings, to be ferried to the task force. Meanwhile some SBS remained behind to prepare charges to sink the ship. They found that the ship was already badly damaged, but placed charges which exploded and sunk the ship after the Sea Kings had returned to pick them up.

[12]

Pebble Island Raid

As the task force approached the islands, the SAS were tasked with attacking the air base on Pebble Island, with the primary intention being to destroy the aircraft on the ground. Pebble Island was close to the approach route planned by the task force, and so the presence of attack aircraft and radar on the island was a source of some concern.

On the 14th of May, the aircraft carrier HMS Hermes, escorted by the destroyer HMS Glamorgan and the frigate HMS Broadsword, headed towards Pebble Island. The only long-range air defence system on the ships was HMS Broadsword's Sea Wolf system, which became defective during the approach. High winds forced HMS Hermes to get within 40 miles of the coast, far closer than planned, so that the two Sea King helicopters could deliver the SAS to the landing zone. As one of the task force's two aircraft carriers, HMS Hermes was a valuable resource, and approaching so close without a long-range air defence system was a significant risk.

The SAS carried 81mm mortars, L1A1 LAWs (Light Anti-armour Weapons), explosive charges, and M16 assault rifles (some with M203 grenade launchers attached). Led to the target by a member of Boat Troop who had previously landed as part of a reconnaissance team, the attackers were able to get to the air base and lay charges on seven aircraft without being detected. Having laid the charges, the attackers opened fire on the aircraft with small arms and LAWs. HMS Glamorgan shelled the air base with her 4.5" gun, directed by a naval gunfire support forward observer that had accompanied the raiding party.

The raid, notably similar to those carried out by the original SAS in the North African desert during World War II, was a complete success. The base was crippled, with all eleven aircraft, the radar installation, ammunition and fuel dumps destroyed. The only British casualties were two men slightly wounded during the withdrawal.

[13]

Operation Plum Duff

To counter the Super Etendards flying from Rio Grande on Tierra del Fuego, British planners looked for a way to insert a special forces team to carry out reconnaissance on the base. The initial plan was to land an SBS team by submarine, but this plan was shelved. Instead, on the night of the 16/17th of May, a stripped-down Sea King was launched from the task force, carrying an SAS team to be inserted onto the Argentinian mainland. The SAS were to report on aircraft operations in preparation for Operation Mikado.

Having had problems navigating in fog, the Sea King landed in Chile, a few kilometres west of the Chile-Argentina border. The SAS patrol set off on foot to complete their mission, which was eventually cancelled. The Sea King crew, meanwhile, attempted to sink the helicopter in a lake, but after failing to do so, had to burn it before giving themselves up to the Chilean authorities. They were returned to the UK, where they were given medals for having carried out numerous dangerous missions. The British Ministry of Defence denied rumours that the helicopter had inserted an SAS team into Argentina, claiming that it had got lost while on an anti-submarine patrol and subsequently had to make an emergency landing.

[14]

Operation Mikado

Operation Mikado was planned to remove the Exocet threat by destroying the missiles and aircraft at their Rio Grande base on Tierra del Fuego.

The main part of the plan called for B Squadron of the SAS to fly from Ascension Island in two C130 Hercules and land on the Rio Grande airfield. Once landed, they would assault the airfield, destroying the aircraft and missiles and killing the pilots. Once this was done, the SAS would escape to Chile, on the C130s if they were still capable of taking off, or on foot otherwise.

Several problems with the plan came to light when rehearsals were carried out on British airfields. The Hercules aircraft would appear on the base's radar well before they arrived, even if they flew very low, and would be an easy target for anti-aircraft fire when they slowed to land. Even if the Argentinians didn't manage to shoot the aircraft down, they would have enough warning to simply block the runways with vehicles.

Because of the high likelihood of failure, and with misgivings being voiced by senior members of B Squadron (including the squadron commander, who was relieved of his command), Operation Mikado was cancelled. Plans for an alternative operation, also involving the SAS, started to be drawn up. This new plan called for an SAS team to be landed on Tierra del Fuego from the submarine HMS Onyx. The SAS would walk to the base, plant explosives to destroy the Super Etendards and Exocets, then escape and evade to Chile. The Argentinian surrender came about before this plan was executed. Although the British had high hopes for this plan's chances of success, they were unaware that the base was guarded by three battalions of marines, which would have made any attack extremely dangerous.

[15]

Sea King Crash

On the 19th of May, a Sea King helicopter carrying SAS troopers from HMS Hermes to HMS Intrepid suffered a bird strike and crashed into the water. 20 members of the SAS, one member of the Royal Signals, and one member of the RAF died in the crash. For the SAS, this was their worst loss in a single incident since World War II.

[16]

San Carlos Water

Although the British intended to land at San Carlos Water on the western edge of East Falkland, HMS Glamorgan was given the task of making the Argentinians believe that they intended to land on the opposite side of the island, near Stanley. To this end, she patrolled off the east coast as far south as Choiseul Sound, and bombarded the east coast near Stanley.

In the early hours of the 21st of May, the British landing force entered San Carlos Water. Twenty-five heavily armed SBS commandos were landed to the east of the Argentinian positions on Fanning Head, and called on the Argentinians to surrender. The Argentinians refused, and so the SBS attacked, with gunfire support from HMS Antrim. The position was taken, meaning that the landing craft were no longer susceptible to attack. Meanwhile, D Squadron of the SAS mounted a diversionary attack on the Darwin garrison, to prevent them moving to attack the landings. This attack, supported by gunfire from HMS Ardent, was so vigorous that the Argentinian commander believed he was being attacked by a battalion (an SAS squadron is roughly the size of an understrength company).

With the SBS and SAS attacks preventing any interference from ground troops, the first wave went ashore at 03:30, one hour later than planned. Aircraft from Goose Green and Argentina attacked the landings several times throughout the day. Despite this, most of 3 Brigade (made up of Royal Marines and paratroopers) were ashore by nightfall. HMS Ardent was sinking after being hit by bombs and cannon fire, and four other ships were damaged. 11 Argentinian aircraft had been shot down by Sea Harriers and anti-aircraft fire.

On the 23rd of May, four A-4B Skyhawks, flown from Argentina, attacked HMS Antelope in San Carlos Water. One was shot down, but two bombs hit. Neither of the bombs detonated, but one later exploded during an attempt to defuse it, causing fires and sinking her the next day. The Argentine Air Force launched more attacks, but caused no damage to British ships. One Argentinian Dagger was shot down by a Sea Harrier, and one Sea Harrier crashed into the sea after bombing Stanley airfield. More aircraft attacked on the 24th of May, leading to British sailors christening the area "Bomb Alley".

[17]

Battle of Seal Cove

On the 22nd of May, an RAF Harrier identified the coastal supply boat ARA Monsunen (a British coaster that had been captured by the Argentinians during the invasion of the islands), which was taking fuel and flour from Fox Bay to Stanley.

The frigates HMS Brilliant and Yarmouth were dispatched to stop ARA Monsunen, and in the early hours of the 23rd of May a Sea Lynx identified her west of Lively Island, about 50 miles southwest of Stanley. A surrender order was radioed to the boat, and an SBS team sent to intercept her, but their helicopter was fired on and had to abort.

When the British ships got to within about four miles, the Argentinian captain decided to beach the boat to fool the British radar, and the crew took shelter on land. The British ships lost contact, and returned to San Carlos. ARA Monsunen's crew returned to her at dawn, but found that her transmission was damaged, and so she had to be towed to Darwin by ARA Forrest, another British ship captured by the Argentinians. ARA Monsunen's cargo was delivered to Stanley on the 25th of May.

[18]

HMS Coventry and SS Atlantic Conveyor

On the 25th of May, Argentina's National Day, HMS Coventry and Broadsword were on duty as radar picket and decoy north of Pebble Island. Skyhawks based in Argentina attacked these ships several times during the day, with the third attack scoring a notable success. HMS Broadsword was hit by a bomb which failed to explode, but which badly damaged her Lynx helicopter. HMS Coventry was hit by two bombs, both of which exploded, and she immediately listed to port. The location of the hits meant that the flooding was uncontrollable, and the order was given to abandon ship. Within 30 minutes she had capsized and sunk.

SS Atlantic Conveyor, a merchant ship owned by Cunard that had been requisitioned for use in the campaign, was with the carrier battle group around 90 miles north-east of Stanley, heading towards San Carlos Water. At around 16:30 she was hit by two Exocet missiles, fired from two Super Etendard fighters. One warhead exploded in the hold where fuel was stowed, causing an uncontrollable fire. Once the fire had subsided the ship was boarded, but nothing could be recovered and the ship was sunk, becoming the first British merchant ship lost to enemy fire since World War II. Six Wessex and three Chinook helicopters were lost on Atlantic Conveyor, which drastically reduced the British ground forces' airlift capability. Consequently, the advance to Stanley was performed largely on foot instead of with the planned helicopter lifts.

[19]

Goose Green

The British commanders had originally intended to bypass Goose Green, but the government wanted a victory on land to counteract the negative impact that ship losses were having on morale back home. On the evening of the 27th of May, three 105mm guns were flown to Camilla Creek House, so that they could provide support to the planned attack. In the evening, 2nd Battalion the Parachute Regiment (2 Para) headed for the start line. The assault was almost called off after the BBC World Service announced, during the planning stages, that 2 Para were preparing to assault Darwin and Goose Green. Fortunately for the British, the Argentinians heard the broadcast but assumed it was a bluff.

Despite an SAS patrol managing to infiltrate the Argentinian positions, the British had little idea of the Argentinian strength or dispositions. 2 Para had around 500 men, supported by three 105mm guns, and were able to call on air and naval gunfire support. The defenders were the 12th Infantry Regiment, with about 800 men, supported by four 105mm guns and several anti-aircraft guns, which were also used in a ground attack role. In addition, they were able to call on air support from Pucará aircraft based at Stanley.

The attack started in the early hours of the 28th of May, and made slow progress before stalling at dawn, as the paras encountered strong Argentinian defences. Lieutenant Colonel "H" Jones tried to lead a company forward to re-invigorate the attack, but was killed doing so. He was posthumously awarded the Victoria Cross for his bravery. The paras resumed their advance late in the morning, when Boca House and Darwin Hill were taken. The advance then continued towards the small airfield and Darwin School, the airfield eventually being taken by a bayonet charge.

As night fell, two Argentinian prisoners of war were sent to the Argentinian commanders with the British terms of surrender, and a deadline of 08:30 the next day. The next morning the Argentinian forces surrendered, and the British government had their victory.

[20]

Many Branch Point

The Argentinian forces at Port Howard on West Falkland were reinforced with a special forces company equipped with British-made Blowpipe man-portable surface-to-air missiles. One of these Blowpipes shot down a British GR3 Harrier and took the pilot prisoner. SAS patrols were inserted onto West Falkland to observe the Argentinian garrisons there. On the 10th of June, an SAS patrol was discovered by an Argentinian patrol at Many Branch Point, near Port Howard. Two men escaped, but one was captured and Captain John Hamilton was killed. After the Argentinian surrender of the Falklands, the Argentinian commander in Port Howard requested that Captain Hamilton be decorated, saying that he was "the most courageous man I have ever seen". Captain Hamilton was posthumously awarded the Military Cross.

[21]

Bluff Cove

Elements of 2 Para had occupied Fitzroy and Bluff Cove, southeast of Stanley, once it was confirmed that there were no Argentinian forces in the area. On the 7th and 8th of June, the Welsh Guards sailed in RFA Sir Tristram and Sir Galahad from San Carlos to Fitzroy and Bluff Cove. Three waves of Argentinian aircraft attacked on the afternoon of the 8th. Three Argentinian aircraft were shot down, with a fourth damaged, but they managed to successfully bomb both RFA Sir Tristram and Sir Galahad. Both ships caught fire and had to be abandoned, at a cost of 56 dead and 150 wounded. RFA Sir Tristram was recovered to the UK and repaired, while RFA Sir Galahad was towed out to sea and sunk as a war grave by HMS Onyx on the 25th of June.

[22]

Mount Harriet

During the week starting on Monday the 31st of May, most of 42 Commando moved to Mount Challenger, where plans were made for an assault on Mount Harriet. The decision was made to attack from the southeast, and extensive patrols were conducted. Some patrols were conducted to the west of the mountain, in an attempt to convince the Argentinian defenders that this would be the direction from which the attack would come. More covert patrols were mounted to the southeast, to find an approach route through the minefields as well as gain information on the strength and dispositions of the Argentinian defenders. During this time, naval gunfire and snipers were used to harass the Argentinians and deny them the chance to sleep.

On the evening of the 11th of June, K and L Companies of 42 Commando moved to their start line southeast of Mount Harriet. Anti-tank missile teams remained near the track leading to Stanley, to guard against any approach by the Argentinian armoured cars based in the capital. J Company were deployed on Wall Mountain, ready to mount a diversionary attack from the west. For over an hour, HMS Yarmouth fired on the defenders with her two 4.5" guns in a preparatory bombardment.

Supported by fire from artillery, mortars, and HMS Yarmouth, the two companies attacking from the southeast advanced up the mountain, remaining undetected until they were very close to the Argentinian positions. The marines then advanced slowly, bunker by bunker, using anti-tank missiles to destroy bunkers. One machine gun position was charged by three corporals, all of whom were awarded the Military Medal.

At dawn, L Company was still fighting on the western side of the mountain, but K Company had secured the eastern side and was moving on to Goat Ridge, between Mount Harriet and Two Sisters. J Company was moving through a minefield to the west, to join their comrades and help finish securing the mountain.

[23]

Mount Longdon

3 Para advanced on foot toward Mount Longdon, and set up a base near Murrell Bridge on the 3rd of June. Both the British and Argentinian forces started aggressive patrolling. One Argentinian patrol managed to capture a radio, leaving open the possibility that 3 Para's radio net was compromised.

The British mistakenly thought that the Argentinian forces had low morale and would put up little resistance. On the night of the 11th of June, the British mounted their attack. The plan was to advance as close as possible to the Argentinian positions under cover of darkness, before storming the trenches with fixed bayonets. However, the Argentinians had planted around 1,500 antipersonnel mines on the approaches. One of the men of B Company stepped on a mine, injuring himself and alerting the Argentinians to the attack.

The resulting hard-fought battle lasted twelve hours. The British commander of 3 Commando, Brigadier Julian Thompson, came close to ordering a retreat. In the end, however, with artillery fire and naval gunfire support from HMS Avenger's 4.5" gun, the British took the mountain. British losses totalled 18 dead and 40 wounded, while the Argentinians lost 31 dead, 120 wounded and 50 taken prisoner. Several decorations were awarded to British paratroopers for actions in the battle, including a posthumous Victoria Cross.

[24]

Two Sisters

45 Commando marched from San Carlos Water towards Mount Kent, where they met SAS patrols on the 4th of June. They then started night patrols towards the Argentinian positions on Two Sisters, leading to several firefights. Losses were taken on both sides, including four British soldiers killed by friendly fire. These patrols gave the British a good idea of the strength and disposition of the Argentinian positions, and an attack was planned for the evening of the 11th of June. The attack was to be initially quiet, with no artillery fire beforehand.

On the evening of the 11th, most of 45 Commando moved to the north of Two Sisters, leaving X Company to the west. X Company started the attack, but by 23:30 they were held up by a determined defence supported by mortars and artillery, and were unable to move further forward. It was decided that a single company would not be sufficient to complete the attack, and so Y and Z companies were brought up, starting their attack at about 00:30. After heavy fighting, during which anti-tank weapons were used extensively to attack Argentinian bunkers, and including a bayonet charge led by a platoon commander from Z Company, 45 Commando were in complete possession of Two Sisters.

On seeing the Argentinian positions in daylight, Lieutenant Colonel Whitehead expressed surprise that the Argentinians had not held their ground, commenting that "With fifty Royals [Royal Marines], I could have died of old age holding this place." Lieutenant Clive Dytor, who had led the bayonet charge, was awarded the Military Cross. Argentinian Private Oscar Ismael Poltronieri, who had held up Y Company with rifle and machine gun fire, was awarded the Argentinian Nation to the Heroic Valour in Combat Cross, the highest Argentinian decoration for bravery.

[25]

Tumbledown

On the morning of the 13th of June, 2nd Battalion Scots Guards were ferried by helicopter from Bluff Cove to Goat Ridge, between Two Sisters and Mount Harriet, and west of Tumbledown, which overlooked Stanley to the east. They were briefed on the planned attack on Tumbledown, to take place that night. Tumbledown was defended by the 5th Marine Infantry Battalion, reinforced by a heavy machine gun company and an artillery battery. The Scots Guards were supported by mortar detachments from other units, a troop of the Blues and Royals (two Scimitar reconnaissance vehicles and two Scorpion light tanks), and naval gunfire support from HMS Active and HMS

Yarmouth, which between them had three 4.5"
guns.

The Argentinians shelled Goat Ridge during the
day, but inflicted minimal casualties. At 19:30, the
British started a bombardment of the Argentinian
positions, and an hour later the reconnaissance
platoon, supported by the Blues and Royals,
mounted a diversionary attack along the Fitzroy-
Stanley track. During a two-hour firefight, one tank
was damaged by a booby trap and two men were
killed, with several wounded during the fight and
subsequent withdrawal through an unmarked
minefield.

At 21:00 G Company started the main assault,
and finding the western end of Tumbledown
undefended, occupied it unobserved. As Left Flank
Company advanced past the peak, however, they
came under heavy fire from machine guns, snipers,
and small arms. The Guards fired back, using L1A1
LAW and Carl Gustav anti-tank rockets against the
Argentinian bunkers. At 02:30 on the 14th of June,
after some very heavy fighting including bayonet
charges, the British took the summit.

Around 06:00 Right Flank Company came up to
attack the positions on the eastern end of
Tumbledown. Following a mass of L1A1 fire, the
guardsmen advanced, and took the positions after

much hard fighting with grenades and bayonets. A counter-attack from Sapper Hill pushed the British back briefly, but was called off by the Argentinian 10th Brigade Chief of Staff.

[26]

Wireless Ridge

Wireless Ridge is a hill close to Stanley which had to be taken before the capital could be attacked. The assault was assigned to 2 Para, with support from a troop of the Blues and Royals, two artillery batteries and naval gunfire support from HMS Ambuscade. The defending unit was the 7th infantry regiment with detachments from other units.

When Lieutenant Colonel Jones, commander of 2 Para, died at Goose Green, the second in command, Lieutenant Colonel David Chaundler, was in England. He joined 2 Para four days after Goose Green. They were ferried by helicopter from Fitzroy to Bluff Cove, where they set up camp. On the morning of the 13th of June, it became clear that

Mount Tumbledown had been taken, so the paratroopers moved to their start positions behind Mount Longdon, leaving everything other than weapons and ammunition at their camp. The mortars and machine guns were delayed by an air attack, but were able to take up their positions later in the day.

The supporting artillery and naval guns fired on the Argentinian positions for 12 hours prior to the attack. D company started the assault late on the 13th of June. They found that C Company of the 7th infantry regiment had withdrawn due to the ferocity of the bombardment. At this point, the Argentinians started a series of attacks, using recoilless rifles, mortars, and rockets.

A and B companies started to advance to the east of D company, but were repulsed. The British machine gunners and the light tanks of the Blues and Royals fired back as the paratroopers retreated. After some time, the Argentinians retreated and the paratroopers took their objective. C company moved up to a position east of Wireless Ridge. D company started the final stage of the assault, initially advancing well, but then they slowed under fierce resistance from A company of the Argentinian 3rd regiment. After two hours of heavy fighting, D company took its objective as the Argentinians ran out of ammunition and retreated.

Two hundred Argentinians made a last-ditch defence near the racecourse, and 50 of them mounted a bayonet charge at the British paratroopers. Their efforts were in vain, however. The charge was stopped by machine gun and artillery fire, and 2 Para held onto their objective.

[27]

Mount William

On Monday the 7th of June, D Company of the Gurkhas sailed from Goose Green to the Fitzroy area. The rest of the battalion were transferred by helicopter over the next couple of days. On the 13th of June, the battalion was helicoptered to a position south of Two Sisters.

As the Scots Guards completed their assault on Mount Tumbledown, the Gurkhas marched along Goat Ridge to their start point, skirting a large minefield and taking some casualties from Argentinian shell fire. On the 14th of June, the Gurkhas were ready to mount a daylight attack on Mount William, but the Argentinians retreated and D Company were able to move onto the summit without facing any opposition.

[28]

Sapper Hill

On the 10th and 11th of June two companies of 40 Commando, along with mortar batteries, were flown to reinforce the Welsh Guards. The Guards were to pass through the Gurkhas once they had taken Mount William, and take Sapper Hill. The Argentinian positions on Sapper Hill were well prepared, with defence in depth, so a hard fight was expected. On the morning of the 14th of June, the marines and Guards started their advance, which was slowed somewhat by a minefield. One company was helicoptered close to the positions, but found that most of the Argentinians had already retreated towards Stanley. After a brief firefight the hill was in British hands.

[29]

Argentinian Surrender

On the 14th of June the British forces, now low on rations and ammunition, were preparing to enter Stanley when a cease-fire was declared. The troops remained outside the town while Lieutenant Colonel Rose of the SAS was helicoptered into Stanley with a small party to meet with General de Brigada Mario Menéndez of the Argentinian army to discuss surrender terms. That morning General Galtieri had ordered the Argentinians to continue the fight. Despite these orders, and the Argentinian Army Code's prohibition of surrender unless more than 50 percent of the men were casualties and 75 percent of the ammunition was spent, the Argentinians surrendered later that day. General Moore flew into Stanley to sign the surrender document for the British. Argentinian officers were allowed to keep their side arms, since there was a real risk that they would by lynched by their men. The time of surrender recorded in the document was backdated to 23:59 GMT (19:59 local time), 14th June 1982. This was done so that the date was the same in both time zones, to avoid confusion.

The next day, one company of Royal Marines crossed over to Port Howard on West Falkland to take the surrender of the two infantry regiments on that island.

On the 20th of June, British forces arrived at Thule in the South Sandwich Islands to remove the Argentinian garrison from the base of Corbeta Uruguay. The garrison surrendered and the base was left unmanned. Some months later, a British warship discovered that the Argentinian flag had replaced the British Union Jack on the flagpole. The British government ordered the buildings on the base to be destroyed and the Union Jack to be run up the flagpole.

[30]

After the Conflict

Within a few days of the surrender, General Galtieri was removed from his position at the head of the junta. Free elections were held the following year, ending 10 years of rule by the military junta. The leaders of the junta were later charged with human rights violations and mismanagement of the conflict. Various members of the junta were jailed, but pardoned in 1989 by President Carlos Menem.

During their occupation of the islands, the Argentinians laid many thousands of land mines, particularly around Stanley. Since the end of the conflict, there have been efforts to mark the minefields and clear the mines. As of 2011, all the minefields are marked. There are an estimated

20,000 mines in 117 minefields covering an area of 13 square kilometres. These minefields have had an unexpected positive environmental impact. Penguins, which are too light to trigger the mines, have taken to making their nests in the minefields, where humans won't disturb them.

During the conflict, the British government commissioned an update of a 1977 report into the Falkland Islands' economy. This report formed the basis of the subsequent economic development and investment in the Islands for the following 20 years.

In Britain, the Conservative government's popularity increased dramatically. They had been trailing the SDP/Liberal alliance in opinion polls before the invasion, but afterwards took the lead by a wide margin, and won a landslide victory in the 1983 general election. The planned cuts to the Royal Navy were cancelled. HMS Endurance stayed in service until 1991, when she was replaced with a newer vessel (originally named HMS Polar Circle, but later renamed HMS Endurance). The sale of HMS Invincible to Australia was cancelled. HMS Hermes was offered instead, with a squadron of Sea Harriers, but the new Australian government decided not to take up the offer. HMS Invincible was decommissioned in 2005, and sold for scrap in

2011. HMS Hermes was decommissioned in 1984 and sold to India in 1986, where she became INS Viraat.

The British government instituted a policy known as "Fortress Falklands", drastically increasing the military presence on the islands. An aircraft carrier was kept on station to provide air cover while Port Stanley airport was improved to allow jet fighters to be temporarily based there. A large new base, RAF Mount Pleasant, was opened in 1985 on East Falkland and became the centrepiece of the newly upgraded Falkland Islands defences. A deep water port for Royal Navy ships was established nearby at Mare Harbour. The RAF base also functions as the islands' international airport, with flights to the UK and Chile. A permanent military presence was established at King Edward Point on South Georgia. This was reduced in the 1990s, and finally wound down completely in 2001.

The UK parliament passed the British Nationality (Falkland Islands) Act, which came into force on 1st January 1983. The act granted full British citizenship to the islanders, thus reversing the effect of the 1981 act. The stated aim of the 1983 act was to clarify the UK's commitment to the islands, and its policy of self-determination for the islanders. In 1985, a new constitution was established for the islands. This was amended in 1997 and replaced in 2009, the 2009 version embedding the right of self-determination within the body of the constitution.

Argentina and Britain did not restore full diplomatic relations until 1990. Argentina has never revoked its claim to the islands, and successive governments have stated that they will continue to pursue the claim via peaceful means. The UK and Falkland Islands governments, however, have consistently refused to enter into talks since 1982, maintaining that there is no issue to resolve. The Argentinian president visited Britain in 1998, when he reaffirmed both Argentina's claim to the islands, and the promise to pursue the matter via peaceful means. In 2001 Tony Blair became the first British prime minister to visit Argentina since the Falklands Conflict, but the issue of the Falkland Islands was not discussed. In 2010, after British companies started drilling for oil off the islands, Argentina asked the United Nations to press Britain to begin talks over the dispute, but Britain refused to enter into talks.

Digital Reinforcements: Free Ebook

To get a free ebook of this title, simply go to www.shilka.co.uk/dcrt and add it to your cart in the normal manner. Then, at checkout, enter discount code DAMN32 to get it free.

The free ebook can be downloaded in several formats: Mobi (for Kindle devices & apps), ePub (for other ereaders & ereader apps), and PDF (for reading on a computer). Ereader apps are available for all computers, tablets and smartphones.

About Russell Phillips

Russell Phillips writes books and articles about military technology and history. His articles have been published in *Miniature Wargames*, *Wargames Illustrated*, and the Society of Twentieth Century Wargamers' *Journal*. Some of these articles are available on his website. He has also been interviewed for the American edition of *The Voice of Russia*.

To get advance notice of new books, join Russell's mailing list at www.rpbook.co.uk/list. Mailing list members get discounts off all of Russell's books, and you can unsubscribe at any time.

Word of mouth is crucial for any author to succeed. If you enjoyed this book, please consider leaving a review where you bought it, or on a site like Goodreads. Even a short review would be very much appreciated.

ALSO BY RUSSELL PHILLIPS

Red Steel: Soviet Tanks and Combat Vehicles of the Cold War

The Bear Marches West: 12 Scenarios for 1980's NATO vs Warsaw Pact Wargames

A Fleet in Being: Austro-Hungarian Warships of WWI

This We'll Defend: The Weapons & Equipment of the U.S. Army

FIND RUSSELL PHILLIPS ONLINE

Website & blog: www.rpbook.co.uk

Twitter: @RPBook

Facebook: facebook.com/RussellPhillipsBooks

Google Plus: +RussellPhillips

E-mail: russell@rpbook.co.uk

Join Russell's mailing list: www.rpbook.co.uk/list

The Forgotten Heroes

The Forgotten Heroes is a UK national charity which is dedicated to working with the carers and families of our wounded or injured servicemen and women. Regardless of conflict or injury, we support families who are learning to live with dramatic changes to their lives which have come about as a result of serving their country. To our knowledge, we are the only charity focussed on supporting the carers of our injured veterans.

We provide varied support for families, and the type of help we provide includes a "buddy" scheme, where carers are provided with a mentor who has been through a similar situation; benefits and financial advice; provision of equipment to make caring easier (such as wet-floor wash rooms, stair lifts and wheelchairs); advocacy and signposting, as well as providing a "champion" to help deal with organisations such as banks and insurance companies, government departments, tribunals etc; and training for family carers to help build their confidence in areas like manual handling and personal care.

The Forgotten Heroes is committed to providing quality information and assistance to help upgrade the quality of life for our heroes and their families. We receive no Government funding, and we are entirely run and staffed by volunteers. Please help us to help those families who have given more than we can ever repay.

E-mail: mail@theforgottenheroes.co.uk

Website: www.theforgottenheroes.co.uk